RUGBY LEAGUE

D0302361

PLAY·THE·GAME

RUGBY
LEAGUE

John Huxley·

Ward Lock Limited · London

© Ward Lock Limited 1989
© Illustrations Ward Lock Limited 1989

First published in Great Britain in 1989
by Ward Lock Limited, 8 Clifford Street,
London W1X 1RB, an Egmont Company

All Rights Reserved. No part of this publication
may be reproduced, stored in a retrieval system,
or transmitted, in any form or by any means,
electronic, mechanical, photocopying, recording,
or otherwise, without the prior permission of the
Copyright owners.

Series editor Ian Morrison
Designed by Cherry Randell

Illustrated by Bob Williams

Text set in Helvetica
by Hourds Typographica, Stafford, England

Printed and bound in Great Britain by
Richard Clay Ltd, Bungay, Suffolk

British Library Cataloguing in Publication Data

Huxley, John, 1947–
  Rugby league.—(Play the game).
  1. Rugby League football – Manuals
  I. Title   II. Series
  796.33′32

  ISBN 0-7063-6766-9

Acknowledgments
The publishers would like to thank the following
people and companies for supplying the
photographs in this book: Allsport (pages 32–3,
42, 60); Mike Brett Photography (page 55);
Colorsport (pages 2, 7, 21); David Howes (page
78), Sporting Pictures (UK) Ltd (page 48) and
Andrew Varley (page 66).

**Frontispiece: Garry Schofield, a world
record signing by Leeds from Hull. He
commanded the £155,000 record fee for his
tremendous try-scoring ability.**

**Overleaf: Martin Offiah the Widnes and
Great Britain winger who was captured
from Rosslyn Park Rugby Union club
pictured playing in the Hong Kong seven-a-
side tournament against New Zealand
before he turned professional.**

CONTENTS

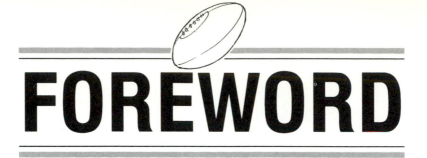

FOREWORD

Rugby League is a fast-growing sport. Each season more new clubs join the thriving leagues organized by the British Amateur Rugby League Association and each winter weekend the professional clubs provide sporting entertainment which is unrivalled in commitment, skill, excitement and crowd appeal.

Rugby League is also essentially a family game, embodying elements which commend it alike to men; women, and, particularly, young people of both sexes. Hundreds of youngsters attend the highly instructive and hugely enjoyable courses operated nationwide by the game's National Coaching Scheme. Many amateur clubs regularly organize sessions of the game's junior version, 'mini-footy', as well as full-scale games for children from the age of seven upwards. Most professional clubs also run extremely lively junior supporters' clubs.

I greatly welcome, therefore, Ward Lock's initiative in producing this book and including the sport of Rugby League in the splendid *Play the Game* series. Those of us closely involved in the game are very conscious of the need to bring its many virtues to a wider audience. This publication is an ideal vehicle for explaining, particularly to youngsters, what Rugby League is all about: its rich heritage; how it is played; and, most importantly, how *you* can become involved in 'the man's game for all the family'.

David Oxley
*Chief Executive of the
Rugby Football League*

The British Amateur Rugby League Association has been described as one of British sport's greatest success stories over the last decade, and not without just cause. The Association has seen an increase in membership of over 20,000 players and 800 teams during this period, half of which have been in the crucial area of Youth Rugby.

Leagues and clubs have now been established on a much wider basis and teams can be found prospering in the Midlands, the West Country, Wales and London, as well as in the north-east of England. The student game has expanded to such an extent that more than thirty teams play regularly in the National Merit Table, with the Oxford and Cambridge Varsity match now in its eighth season.

A game which was once very parochial is also extending its international boundaries, and foreign tours are now the order of the day. Indeed, since BARLA's formation in 1973 there have been as many as fourteen tours to and from the South Pacific, seven in each direction. Rugby League has also established its own very successful National Coaching Scheme.

The aim of BARLA is to make amateur Rugby League football a truly national sport by 1995, the centenary year of the game, and we are sure that this excellent publication will play an important role in helping us achieve that objective.

Maurice Oldroyd
*National Administrator of the
British Amateur Rugby League Association*

HISTORY & DEVELOPMENT OF RUGBY LEAGUE

While the origins of football are lost in the mists of time, Rugby League can proudly point to its birthday: 29 August 1895. The date marks the second of two important breakaways from primitive football, which in England in the early nineteenth century was played according to various sets of rules and was usually a scrimmaging, kicking and mauling game in which two teams of players tried to force the ball into their opponents' goal or across an agreed boundary line.

At Rugby School the boys played a non-handling version of the game, and the first break with tradition occurred in 1823 when a pupil called William Webb Ellis picked up the ball and ran with it. Two codes of football then began to evolve: in the Rugby version, the players handled and ran with an oval ball; in the other version, now known as soccer, they kicked a round ball.

The English Rugby Football Union was formed in 1871, and by 1893 had attracted some 400 member clubs. By then, however, a North-South divide was making itself felt. The Rugby Football Union held fast to its belief in the spirit of amateurism, but the harsh reality of life in the industrial North of England made it difficult to adhere to that code and make a living at the same time.

In those days men used to work in mills, mines and factories all through Saturday to make a living wage for themselves and their families. If they took Saturday afternoon off to play Rugby football they lost money and their families suffered. To encourage them to take time off work some clubs wanted to pay what was known as 'broken time'. The argument was that they were not paying wages, which was strictly against the amateur principle, but giving compensation for missing a valuable shift at work.

The rulers of the Union game were afraid that if they gave in to the Northern clubs on the issue of broken time, they would be opening the door to professionalism. Pressure for change built up in the North and, on 20 September 1893, the inevitable clash between the two factions took place at the Rugby Union's annual meeting in London.

Two Yorkshire club representatives, Mr J. A. Millar and Mr M. Newsome, proposed: 'Players are to be allowed compensation for *bona-fide* loss of time.' The motion was lost by 418 votes to 136, but there was enough

HISTORY · & · DEVELOPMENT

support to create a body of clubs who met regularly to discuss their predicament. Sufficient progress was made to call a meeting of Northern clubs at the George Hotel, Huddersfield on 29 August 1895 to discuss the situation.

A gentleman from the West Yorkshire town of Brighouse, Mr H. H. Waller, presided over the meeting, made up of representatives from Batley, Bradford, Brighouse, Broughton Rangers (Salford), Dewsbury, Halifax, Huddersfield, Hull, Hunslet, Leeds, Leigh, Liversedge (Huddersfield), Manningham (Bradford), Oldham, Rochdale Hornets, St Helens, Tyldesley (Leigh), Warrington, Wakefield, Widnes and Wigan.

Only one of the representatives, the gentleman from Dewsbury, voted against the proposition that the clubs resign from the Rugby Union and form their own Northern Rugby Union and so be able legally to pay their players broken-time expenses. Once it became known that the split had been made, two more clubs, Stockport and Runcorn, joined the breakaway band. A period of furious work followed but, by Saturday 7 September 1895, the new code was ready with its first set of fixtures.

Retribution was not long in coming. The Rugby Union forbade its member clubs to play against any from the Northern Union, and introduced even stricter rules against payments to players. The Northern Union, out on their own, began to develop their game. Broken-time rates were set at six shillings (30p) and several of the wealthier clubs set a pattern for the future by paying their better players slightly more than the basic rate.

By the first annual meeting in 1896, the Northern Union had 59 member teams. Among the new arrivals the following season were present-day League members Bramley, Castleford, Salford and Swinton. The next major event was the introduction of the Northern Union Cup, the forerunner of today's Challenge Cup. It was a knock-out competition and in the first final, played at

Headingley in 1897, Batley, nicknamed the Gallant Youths, beat St Helens 10-3 before a crowd of almost 14,000. At this stage the Northern Union was still playing under Rugby Union laws but, at the end of the second season, the first signs of a real split appeared.

To make the Northern Union game more attractive to spectators, it was decided to make various changes. The points value for scoring was altered so that every type of goal counted as two points and the line-out was eliminated. These changes were followed in 1906 by one of the main features that separates Rugby League from the Union game, the reduction to 13 men a side – a move designed to open up the game by cutting down on the number of forwards. The idea was an immediate success and another distinguishing feature was then introduced: after each completed tackle there would be a two-man scrum or play-the-ball.

Batley retained the Challenge Cup in 1898 before a massive crowd of 27,941 at Headingley, beating their close West Yorkshire rivals Bradford. The players noted the huge attendance and called for the abolition of broken-time expenses and the introduction of full professionalism. Their argument was accepted by the 1898 annual meeting and professional players have been a fundamental part of the senior section of the game ever since. With money being paid openly, the creation of more successful teams became important and the search for top players moved outside the North into Rugby Union strongholds such as South Wales, the South-West and North-East of England.

Until 1900 the Northern Rugby Union ran two county leagues, one each in Lancashire and Yorkshire, and the Challenge Cup. In 1901 the first combined league of the game's top clubs was brought into operation with 12 clubs: Batley, Bradford, Broughton Rangers, Halifax, Huddersfield, Hull, Hunslet, Oldham, Runcorn, Salford, Swinton and Warrington.

The competition was called the Northern Rugby League. Later it was agreed to take the winners of a play-off between the winners of the county competitions into the new league each season giving the Northern Union an early form of promotion and relegation. Such was the success of the 'super league' that attendances at the county games fell and this led to a fall in the number of clubs the following season.

Again the Northern RU was forced to adapt and, for season 1902–03, it was decided to introduce a two-division system with a first and second section each of 18 clubs. This did not last long and in 1905 one large league was created.

It was not long before the new Northern Union code became attractive to other Rugby-playing nations. During the 1905 New Zealand All Black tour to Britain a member of their party, winger George W. Smith, met Northern Union officials and players. He was so impressed with what he saw that he agreed to recruit a party of New Zealand players to return to Britain as a touring team and play as professionals.

Back home Smith and another enthusiast, Albert Henry Baskerville, succeeded in collecting enough players to mount a tour to Great Britain in 1907–08. While they were making the arrangements for the trip they received a cable from a group of Australians interested in their scheme. They agreed to play three exhibition games under Union laws in Australia on their way to Britain, and recruited top Australian player Herbert Henry 'Dally' Messenger in consequence. They had also acquired a nickname, the 'All Golds', bestowed on them by fellow New Zealanders who disapproved of them leaving the Union ranks and accepting money for playing Rugby.

The tourists arrived in Britain in October 1907. They played their first 13-a-side match at Bramley and won. A win over Huddersfield followed. But the English teams were beginning to get their measure and Wigan became the first club to beat them. A series of defeats together with the news that they had been suspended for life by the New Zealand Union did little to lift the tourists' spirits and in the historic first Northern Union Test at Headingley on 25 January 1908 they were defeated 14-6.

The result might have been predictable but the British sporting public were still curious about this new-style touring team and, for the second Test at Chelsea's Stamford Bridge ground in London, 15,000 turned up to watch as the All Golds levelled the series with an 18-6 victory. The scene switched to Cheltenham and the deciding Test which went to the Australasian tourists 8-5.

As in modern Rugby League, the touring players who did well became targets for success-hungry British clubs. Winger George Smith signed for Oldham and one of the most popular players, half-back Lance Todd, who was later to have an important role in the game's development as an administrator and journalist, joined Wigan. The returning All Golds played three more games in Australia on the way home, this time under Northern Union laws. This encouraged the New South Wales Rugby Union to break away and form their own Rugby League and, by a casting vote, adopt the Northern Union laws.

The game was now in place in Australia and that proved to be a major breakthrough for the new code. In 1908, a year after the New Zealanders, the first Australian touring team sailed for Britain. Today's intense Test match rivalry between the two countries had its beginnings at Queen's Park Rangers ground in London. The result was a thrilling 22-22 draw, although the crowd of 2,000 was disappointing. For the second Test the Northern Union continued its policy of staging its big matches at 'propaganda' centres, in an attempt to spread the game. This time, at St James's Park, Newcastle-upon-Tyne, there were 22,000 spectators and they saw the Northern Union win 15-5. The crunch Third Test was played at Villa Park, Birmingham and, although the British won the match and the series, a very disappointing attendance made the event an anti-climax. At the end of the tour the British clubs swooped again and a number of players decided to stay, including winger Albert Rosenfeld who joined Huddersfield. In 1913–14 he scored 80 tries in the season – a record that still stands.

While the game was spreading overseas, the Northern Union was still trying to break out of its main stronghold and in 1908 Barry, Aberdare, mid-Rhondda and Treherbert were admitted to join two other Welsh clubs, Ebbw Vale and Merthyr Tydfil.

After receiving two sets of tourists, the Northern Union ventured out of the UK for the first time in 1910 and travelled to Australia and New Zealand. For the first Test on Australian soil there was a fantastic 42,000 crowd in Sydney and the British won 27-20. The two met again in Brisbane and again the British tourists came out on top, 22-17. The Australians, however, have never recognized this match as an official Test; although they played several New Zealanders in their teams for two later matches, one of which they won and the other they drew, they preferred to include these matches in their official records. Britain v Australia at sport never seems the same without a disagreement!

The new code of Rugby League was established. Virtually all connections with its Union parentage had gone, apart from those individual players who crossed British sport's greatest divide. Competition was suspended from 1915 until 1919 because of the First World War, then there followed a major boom in Northern Union's popularity as a spectator sport.

Two years later the game chose its modern identity. Delegates at the 1922 annual meeting decided to ditch the localized name of Northern Union and adopt a new all-embracing label of Rugby Football League. In 1927 the Challenge Cup final, Oldham v Swinton at Wigan, was broadcast

for the first time on radio. Two years later, following much argument, came a major change in policy: the Cup final moved to London and its spiritual home, Wembley. The first Wembley final was between mighty Wigan and little Dewsbury from West Yorkshire. Wigan won 13-2, and the big crowd of 41,500 vindicated the decision to move the game south. Now Rugby League Cup final day is a traditional high spot on the British sporting calendar even though the game is not a major part of the southern scene – yet!

The French and Rugby go naturally together, especially in the south-west of their country. In 1933, at a time when the French were suspended from the international Union game on charges of professionalism, they sent a delegation to meet English League officials. As a direct result of those talks the 1933-34 Australian tourists played an exhibition game against Great Britain at Stade Pershing in Paris. There was a crowd of 20,000 and they saw the Kangaroos win 63-13 on a frozen pitch.

The French had acquired the taste for Rugby League and, led by Jean Galla, a former French Union international, a number of other players were persuaded to switch codes and tour Britain. They won just one of their matches but they were inspired to develop the game in their country. In April 1934 the Fédération Française de Jeu à Treize (game for 13) was launched and in 1935 a tri-cornered European championship with England and Wales was created.

Since their admission to the code the French had been pushing hard for a World Cup competition. After the Second World War they at last got their wish and staged the first-ever tournament in 1954; much to everyone's surprise, a weakened British team were the winners! The Lions team were led by a former Scots Rugby Union player Dave Valentine, who played for Huddersfield. In recognition of their contribution to the sport, games against the French were elevated to Test match status in 1957.

In the post-war sports boom in Britain, Rugby League was still trying to expand outside its North of England heartland. In 1952 the Challenge Cup final was televised nationally for the first time.

The League decided to try a two-division format again for 1962–63, but the experiment lasted just two seasons; Swinton won the championship each time. In 1964 substitutes were allowed for the first time. They could be used to replace injured players, but only until half-time. A year later the League gave the go-ahead for replacement players to be allowed for any reason up to and including the interval. The same year, 1965, the English Schools Rugby League was formed.

For some years Rugby League had been seeking ways to make itself more attractive to spectators. It was felt that the law allowing one team to hold possession for as long as it could was detracting from the spectacle. So, in 1966, a limit of four successive tackles was imposed. After a team had reached that limit they either had to kick the ball or concede possession to a scrummage. In 1972 the limit was extended to six tackles.

Another major change was to play matches on a Sunday. The experiment was started in 1967 and soon Sunday became the normal match-day for the professional code. In 1969 substitutes were allowed at any stage in the match, and Universities Rugby League was introduced. In 1971 the prestigious John Player competition was launched, and the following year a strange new sound wafted over league grounds. Match time-keeping was taken away from the referees and handed over to two club officials, one from each side, who signalled half-time and the end of a match with a hooter.

A third attempt to make two divisions work was started in 1973, and this time the League, despite constant opposition from some clubs, have stayed with the system. Amateur Rugby League had reached a major crisis point, however. The number of leagues and clubs had fallen so dramatically that the grass-roots game virtually died. Alarmed by this situation a group of enthusiasts met in Huddersfield to form the British Amateur Rugby League Association (BARLA) who took control of that side of the game. At first the new amateur body was not recognized by the professionals, but once it was seen that BARLA, as the new body was known, could handle its own affairs, peace was restored and recognition granted.

A new end-of-season knock-out competition, the Premiership, was launched in 1975. Today the top eight clubs face each other after the end of the League competition. The top four take home venue then the other four are drawn against them. The system was introduced to the second division in 1987.

In 1978 the game expanded internationally for the first time since the French were admitted in the 1930s when Papua New Guinea were granted full international board status. The game had been taken to that far-off land by Australian servicemen during the Second World War and it has become their national sport.

A controversial development in 1983 was the sin bin. Under this system players can be sent off for spells of either five or ten minutes and then can return to the action. British Rugby League has never felt happy with the sin bin, although Australia and New Zealand, who suggested the idea, remain in favour of it. In the same year the value of the try was up-rated from three to four points and a new law was introduced making players hand the ball over if they still had it after six completed, successive tackles. In 1988 a further change came in, designed to speed up the game still further. Australian-inspired, it forced players in possession after five tackles to keep the ball in play rather than end the action.

Rugby League is generally considered to be a professional sport. Although this is true of one small part of the game, many people in Britain who live outside the North of England do not seem to realize that far more amateurs play Rugby League than professionals.

There are around 1,300 professional players in the British League but more than 25,000 amateur players who, week in and week out, play the game just for fun. Although there are an increasing number of full-time professional players in the game, particularly the Australian and New Zealand stars who are recruited by British clubs, the vast majority are part-time professionals. That means that they have day-time jobs and are paid to play and train. In the Northern Rugby League, the correct name for the professional competition, there are 34 professional clubs in two divisions, 14 in the first and 20 in the second. In the first division each club plays each other twice on a home and away basis to decide the League championship; in the second division there are so many clubs that the fixture formula is more complicated. Clubs do not face all the others in the division – just a selection.

The top League in the world is not in Britain but in Australia. It is called the Sydney Premiership although it now includes teams from outside the Sydney area – as far into Queensland as Brisbane. They have developed the game to a very high professional level and their players, while still being to a large extent semi-professional, have seen their game become a science. It is the premier game in both New South Wales and Queensland and is also played to a lesser extent in the other states, where Australian Rules football is bigger.

The Sydney competition finishes in a Grand Final at the end of the season. The clubs play in a League for the majority of the season and the top five clubs are then included in a series of semi-finals and finals, and the two survivors qualify for the Grand Final. This is one of the major events in world rugby.

In New Zealand the game is played on an amateur basis and takes second place behind the national game of Rugby Union. League has developed rapidly under the influence of the Australian game and the Kiwis produce some of the best players in the world. Unfortunately for New Zealand, most of these players have to go either to Australia or the UK to pursue a career as professionals but they still take great pride in wearing their black and white strip when they play for the national side which is now a formidable force.

French Rugby League has suffered a decline in recent years and they are working hard to inspire a revival. The game is mainly played in the south-west corner of the country although there are amateur sides in Paris.

Papua New Guinea's Test team is called after an exotic bird, the Kumuls, and their fast, open brand of football has been winning them friends throughout the League world. Now the game is spreading through the South Pacific islands and its future in that region is looking particularly bright.

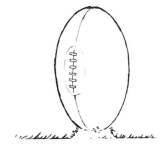

EQUIPMENT &
TERMINOLOGY

The pitch

Rugby League is played on a grass surface. The pitch is rectangular and must not be longer than 100m (109yd) and 68m (74yd) wide. The in-goal areas at either end of the pitch may vary in depth from 6–11m (6–11yd). Most Leagues and competitions define the minimum size of pitch acceptable to them; smaller pitches may be laid out for

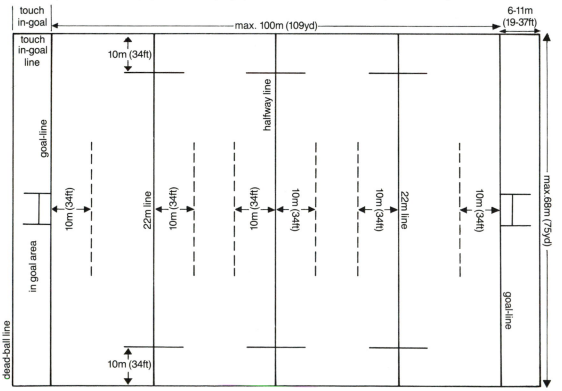

schoolboy games.

The boundary lines down the 'long' side of the pitch are called touch-lines and those joining the outer corners of the in-goal areas are the dead-ball lines.

Three major parallel lines divide the playing area approximately into quarters. In the middle is the centre-line which marks the boundary of each team's territory; kick-offs are taken from the centre spot on this line. At the far end of each half is the goal-line, where the goal-posts stand. In between the centre-line and the goal-line is the 22-metre line; this is still more commonly known by its pre-metrication name, the '25', when it was drawn 25yd (22.8m) from the goal-line.

Ten metres on either side of the centre-line is a short broken line which marks the limit for defending teams when they are receiving a kick-off; another broken line, 10m (formerly 10yd) from the 22, marks the limit for players receiving a drop-kicked re-start taken from the 22.

A third short broken line is marked 10m (formerly 10yd) from the goal-line in front of the goal-posts. Running parallel with the touch-lines are broken 10m lines which cross the centre and each 22 line. These mark the limits for scrummage after the ball has been kicked into touch.

The ball

Rugby League, like Rugby Union, is played with an oval-shaped ball. The outer casing

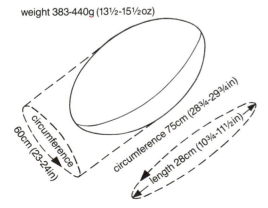

weight 383-440g (13½-15½oz)

circumference 60cm (23-24in)

circumference 75cm (28¾-29¾in)

length 28cm (10¾-11½in)

should be made of leather or a similar material which can be inflated. It should weigh, when dry and clean, 383–440g (13½–15½oz) and measure 58–61cm (23–24in) at its widest circumference, 28–29cm (10¾–11½in) in length and 73–75cm (29–29¾in) at its longest circumference. If the ball deflates during the game the referee has to stop the game and swap it for another.

The goal-posts

One of the most distinctive features of any Rugby pitch is the pair of H-shaped goal-posts. There are strict rules governing their shape and size. They consist of two

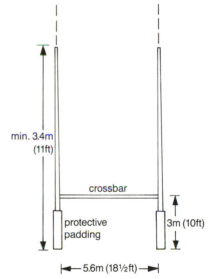

min. 3.4m (11ft)

crossbar

protective padding

3m (10ft)

5.6m (18½ft)

upright posts joined together by a crossbar, and are positioned on the goal-line at an equal distance from each touch-line. A goal may be scored when the ball goes through the uprights above the crossbar; to help the officials decide whether the ball has passed through the posts correctly, the uprights are considered to extend indefinitely upwards. To protect the players from injuring themselves against an upright, most clubs now bind the bottom of each upright with rubber pads.

The uprights, which may be made of wood

This is how a Rugby League player dresses for the game.

or tubular metal, must be more than 3.4m (11ft) high and 5.6m (18½ft) apart with the crossbar a minimum of 3m (10ft) off the ground.

Flag-posts

Flag-posts are placed at the junction of the goal-lines and touch-lines. Made of a non-rigid material, they should not be more than 1.25m (4ft) high.

Players' equipment

All players in a team must wear the same colour of jersey, socks and shorts. The jerseys are usually numbered to indicate the players' positions. If there is a clash in the teams' colours the referee can instruct either team to change to an alternative, distinctive strip; generally, it is the away team which has to change colours. On their feet players wear the type of boot which suits their position on the field. Most forwards choose a high-sided boot which provide support for the ankle, while most back-division players prefer a lighter, shoe-type boot. Studs in the sole of the boot are permitted but they must not have a diameter of more than 8mm (⁵⁄₁₆in) at the apex. They may vary in length to suit the pitch conditions but they must not be dangerous to other players. Before each match the referee or the touch-judges will inspect the studs to ensure that they are safe. Shoulder pads are allowed as long as they do not contain any rigid materials, and quite a number of modern professionals use head-guards or strips of tape to protect their ears.

The standard numbering system in the British game is:

1 – Full-back
2 – Right wing
3 – Centre three-quarter
4 – Centre three-quarter
5 – Left wing
6 – Stand-off half
7 – Scrum-half
8 – Open-side prop
9 – Hooker
10 – Blind-side prop
11 – Second-row forward
12 – Second-row forward
13 – Loose forward
14 – Back-division substitute
15 – Forward substitute

In Australia and New Zealand the fowards are numbered 13 to 8 instead of 8 to 13. They also call the stand-off half the five-eighth and the loose forward a lock.

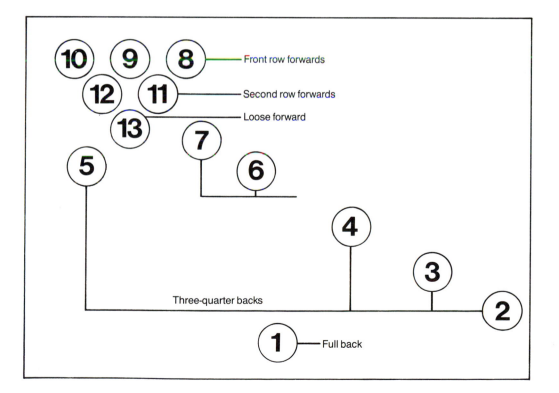

Front row forwards
Second row forwards
Loose forward
Three-quarter backs
Full back

RUGBY LEAGUE · TERMINOLOGY

Acting half-back   A player who stands behind the ball carrier when he is tackled and then plays the ball.

Advantage   Referees can allow play to continue if it is to the advantage of the team who has not committed the offence or infringement.

Back   A member of a team who plays as a half-back, three-quarter or full-back.

Ball back   If the ball goes into touch without bouncing, it is returned to the point where it was kicked and play re-starts with a scrummage to the opposing team.

Blind side   If the play is taking place near one side of the field, the shorter side to the touch-line is known as the blind-side.

Broken play   When play is taking place outside a set-piece situation, e.g. a scrummage.

Caution   Warning a player receives if the referee decides that his personal foul or persistent infringing has to be officially noted in his notebook for recording to the League disciplinary authority.

Charge down   This happens when a player kicks the ball and a defender knocks it down.

Converting a try   The act of kicking a goal after a try has been scored.

Cover tackle   Tackling an attacking player who has broken through the defensive line.

Crossing   The act of deliberate obstruction by attacking players. The passer continues

running into the path of would-be tacklers to protect his team-mate. Known as 'shepherding' in Australia. This is an infringement.

Dead ball   Any ball that goes out of play.

Differential penalty   After a technical infringement at a scrummage the referee awards a penalty but it does not entitle the non-offending team to kick for goal and score. They have the option to kick for touch or tap to re-start.

Drop goal   The scoring of a goal from open play by means of a drop kick. Known as a field goal in Australia.

Drop kick   A kick made by dropping the ball from the hands and making contact with the foot as soon as the ball hits the ground.

Drop out   A means of bringing the ball back into play. It is a drop kick taken from either between the posts or from the centre of the '22'.

Dummy   An attacking player holds the ball after pretending to pass it with the object of deceiving the defenders.

Dummy half   see *Acting half-back*.

Feeding the scrum   When the scrum-half places the ball into the tunnel between the two sets of forwards at a scrummage. Feeding is also a term used to describe an infringement at the scrummage when scrum-halves deliberately slant the ball in to their own forwards' feet.

Free kick   The kick awarded to a team which kicks into touch from a penalty. Taken 10m (11yd) opposite where the ball crosses the touch-line, it can be kicked in any direction but you cannot score from it.

Forward   A player who operates in the

scrummage.

Forward pass   An infringement when a player throws the ball forward towards his opponents' goal-line.

Full-time   The end of a game after 80 minutes.

Hand over   When a team has retained the ball for six tackles and is then forced to give the ball to their opponents.

Heel   When a player pushes the ball behind himself with his heel or boot sole.

Hook   When a hooker pulls the ball back in the scrummage.

Kick-off   When the match is started with a kick from the centre spot.

Knock-on   An infringement when a player knocks the ball towards his opponents' goal-line with his arm or hand.

Loose arm   An offence when the hooker packs down in the scrum with one arm not correctly bound round the prop forward.

Loose ball   When the ball is not held by a player or being scrummaged.

Loose head   The prop-forward nearest the referee at a scrummage.

Mark   The point from which a penalty is taken, or where a scrum is formed.

Obstruction   When a player deliberately impedes an opponent not in possession of the ball.

Offside   A law applied when a player is temporarily out of the play and may be penalized if he joins in the game.

Onside   Used when a player is not offside.

Open side   The side of the scrum or play-the-ball on the far side from the touch-line. Opposite to *Blind side*.

On the full   Used when the ball crosses any line without bouncing.

Pack   A common term used to describe one team's forwards.

Pass   Throwing the ball from one player to another.

Penalize   When the referee awards a penalty kick against an offending player.

Penalty kick   A type of free kick awarded to the non-offending team after an offence has been committed.

Place kick   Describes a kick where the ball is placed on the ground before being kicked.

Play-the-ball   The way to bring the ball back into play after a tackle is completed.

Punt   Kicking the ball from the hands without it hitting the ground.

Put-in   see *Feeding the scrum*.

Ruck   A group of players contesting possession.

Scrum, Scrummage or Scrimmage   The two sets of forwards directly facing each other to contest possession.

Second movement   When a grounded player reaches over the goal-line after he has been tackled to touch the ball down.

Sin bin   Where a player is sent after being temporarily dismissed.

Spot tackling   The system of man-to-man marking when defenders take one of their opponents as a special responsibility.

Stealing   The act of taking the ball from a player before the tackle is called as complete.

Strike   The action of a hooker attempting to pull the ball back with his feet in the scrum.

Tap kick   When a team opts for tapping the ball on a kicker's boot to re-start the game. The ball can travel in any direction, and any player, including the kicker, may gather the ball.

Touch-down   When a defending player grounds the ball in his own in-goal area.

Touch in-goal   When a player steps outside the pitch limits while in the in-goal area.

Try   The act of grounding the ball in the in-goal area for a score.

Upright tackle   Describes a tackle when both players remain on their feet.

Voluntary tackle   A rare happening when a player in possession voluntarily stops play without an effective tackle having taken place.

Wally Lewis the Australian stand off half and captain. One of the greatest players ever produced by his country.

THE GAME – A GUIDE

Rugby League is a game designed for two teams of players each with thirteen players on the pitch at any one time. Each team must be dressed in separate, different-coloured outfits. Substitutes, two per team, are allowed and they can be utilized at any time in the game. In Britain teams are allowed to make four changes during the match; other countries have their own local laws governing substitutes. Usually the substitutes are a forward and a half-back or three-quarter. In a match the Number 14 jersey is worn by a player who is designated as a replacement for the back division and the Number 15 for a forward.

The game is governed by a series of laws, and a referee assisted by two touch-judges is responsible for enforcing them during a match. In both codes of Rugby, League and Union, players are noted for their acceptance of refereeing decisions; dissent is not acceptable behaviour.

The object of any game of Rugby League is to score more points than the opposing side. Players carry the oval-shaped ball towards their opponents' end of the pitch by passing the ball with their hands to team-mates or kicking it. There are two ways to score: a try or a goal. A try is scored when a player crosses the opposing team's goal-line and grounds the ball.

A team receives four points for scoring a try no matter where the ball is grounded in the in-goal area. After a try the scoring team is then allowed to go for two extra points by kicking the ball off the ground from a point level with the place it was grounded. The extra points are awarded if the ball goes between the posts and over the crossbar, in what is known as a conversion.

There are two other varieties of goal. At any time during open play a player may drop the ball on the ground and, once it has bounced, kick it through the upper half of the posts. This is known as a drop goal and it is worth one point. There is also the penalty goal. This is awarded if a player is judged to have committed a personal foul against an opponent or a technical infringement of the laws. The only time that does not apply is when the referee awards a differential penalty which is given for an infringement of a scrummage law. In Rugby League a penalty goal is worth two points and is scored by kicking the ball off the ground and over the crossbar.

Play in senior Rugby League matches lasts for 80 minutes, divided into two equal halves, with a five-minute interval between the two. A team captain, a player nominated by the club at professional level or elected by the other players in amateur teams, will meet his opposite number just before the start of a match. Watched by the referee, they will toss a coin to decide who kicks off. The home captain tosses and the away captain 'calls'. The winner chooses which end to defend first while the loser kicks off.

The referee, who is usually dressed in black or wears a uniform designated by the ruling League, starts the game by blowing a whistle when he is satisfied that both teams are ready to start the game. He must not wear any colour that clashes with the players and it is quite common in Rugby League to see a referee wear a red, yellow, green or white shirt.

The referee has a very responsible job. He is in charge of the game and must ensure that the laws are obeyed and that maximum consideration is given to the safety of the players. He starts and stops the game with a whistle. In the professional game he receives a signal from two time-keepers at the side of

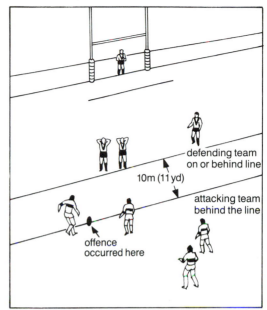

Paying the penalty. This is what happens when a penalty kick is taken.

It'a try! A player dives over the line to put the ball down for four points.

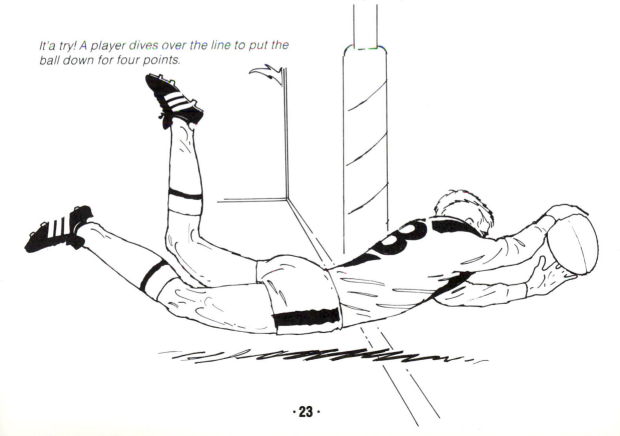

RUGBY LEAGUE

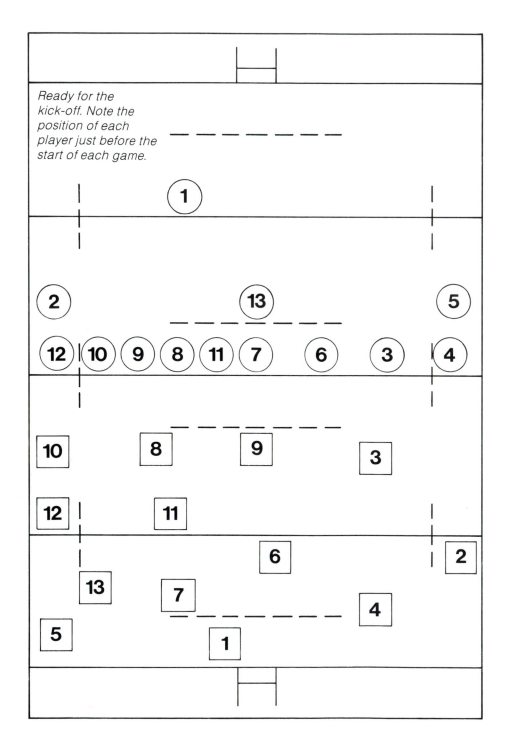

Ready for the kick-off. Note the position of each player just before the start of each game.

Play-the-ball. One of Rugby League's vital skills.

the pitch when it is half-time and when the game is completed. In the amateur game the referee generally controls time-keeping and at least one reliable watch is an essential part of his equipment. He also carries a notebook to record the score and official cautions of players for breaches of discipline.

Referees are assisted in most matches by two touch-judges. They each have a flag, usually one red and one orange, and their job is to mark the place on the edge of the pitch where the ball passes out of play, mark the 10-metre point at penalty situations and assist the referee by observing players' behaviour when they are out of the referee's vision. After a try or following the award of a penalty, the touch-judges have to stand behind the goal posts; if the ball goes correctly between the posts, they hold their flags up, and if the kick fails they wave them close to the ground.

All 13 players must be in their correct half of the pitch before a game can start. The player who takes the kick-off has to make sure that the ball goes 10m (34ft) into his opponents' half and stays on the pitch. If he fails on either count, his opponents receive a penalty kick on the centre spot from which they can score – if they have a player who can kick that far!

Usually a player will direct his starting kick across to one of the wings. The opposing team's set of six forwards try to position themselves under where the ball will land while the kicker's forwards charge at them trying either to take the ball themselves or prevent the receiving players from starting an attack.

There are two distinct phases of play in Rugby League. A team either has possession of the ball or it is defending. Let us now run through an imaginary game so that the significance of the two phases can be fully understood. After the kick-off from the centre spot the defending players catch the ball. The player in possession can run forward, attempt to break through the defence and then, at any stage while he is making progress, pass the ball to one of his team-mates. But he is restricted to passing the ball backwards and in *no* other direction. If the referee thinks he has passed forward deliberately he can award a penalty.

The defending players can try to stop the ball carrier by tackling him to the ground. A tackle can be made in any way a defender chooses, with the following restrictions:

1 Only the ball carrier can be tackled.
2 A tackle must be made below the head.
3 A ball carrier cannot be tripped.
4 No blow must be made with the fist or any other foul tactic used.

Once a ball carrier is taken to the ground or his progress is stopped completely he has to play-the-ball to restart play. Should there be any doubt or confusion the referee will call 'Held' to indicate that the tackle is complete. If the ball carrier's team retain possession for four more play-the-balls they are then faced with a decision.

If they hold on for one more tackle, and a player *is* tackled, then they must hand the ball over to their opponents. Regaining possession is obviously difficult. The alternative to risking another tackle is a long kick upfield, which will certainly keep the opposing team deep in their own half, and could possibly lead to them making an error.

Players will evade the tacklers for as long as possible to avoid being stopped. They can move the ball around with passes and, once a gap in the defence is created, send one of their team through to attempt a score. The only time that the game is ever halted is when a player in possession infringes a law or after foul play.

For technical offences the referee awards a scrummage to re-start the game. This is when six forwards bind together in a triangular shape and the front row of three inter-lock their heads with their opposing numbers. The ball is fed into the gap between them with possession going to the side whose hooker can pull the ball into their side.

Like soccer, the game of Rugby League has its offside law. Although it appears quite complicated at first, it is basically quite simple. When the game requires a play-the-ball, i.e. after a completed tackle, the defending side must be five metres away or they are offside. A player is also offside if he seeks to gain an advantage by interfering in front of his team when they are holding the ball.

At the start of the second half the teams switch direction and play continues until the time-keepers or referee decide that the 80 minutes have been completed. If players are injured and the referee has to stop the game, the time it takes either to remove the player

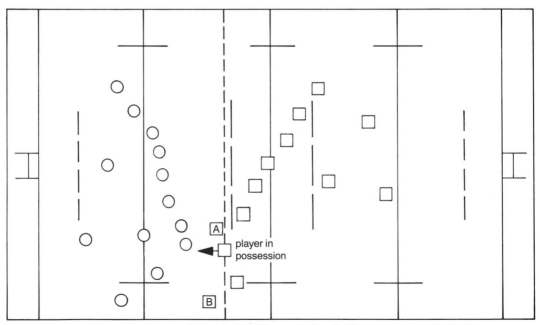

Caught out! Player 'B' is offside

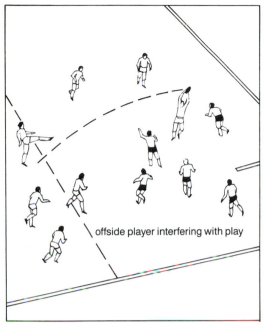

offside player interfering with play

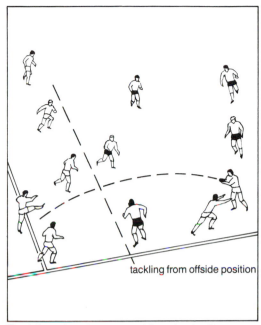

tackling from offside position

The player catching his teammate's kick is offside.

Tackling the player catching the ball in advance of the kicker is offside.

from the pitch or complete his treatment is added on at the end of each half. If a penalty is awarded and then the hooter or whistle is sounded, the non-offending side can take the kick.

In addition to breaching the laws a player can be penalized by the referee for bad behaviour. There is a code of ten offences that players must not commit and they are:

1 Tripping or striking another player.
2 Attacking an opponent's head when making a tackle.
3 Dropping the knees on a player who is on the ground.
4 Using a dangerous throw, e.g. of a martial arts kind, in a tackle.
5 Deliberately breaking the Laws of the Game.
6 Using offensive language.
7 Disputing the decision of the referee or touch-judges.
8 Re-entering the field of play after a temporary absence without permission of the referee or touch-judge.
9 Behaving against the spirit of the game.
10 Deliberately obstructing an opponent who is not in possession.

If a player is penalized for any of the above breaches of behaviour the referee can award a penalty against his team which would cost them points if the opposition kick the goal. Or he may send the offending player to the sin bin for five or ten minutes and that would leave the team short of men. Or he could send the player from the pitch completely and he would then have to appear before the League disciplinary committee who would probably suspend him.

Kicking plays an important part in modern Rugby League. Although it is essentially a handling game and by far the largest part of it is spent in passing the ball, the science of kicking the oval ball is nevertheless an important part of a team's armoury.

RUGBY LEAGUE

The ball cannot be kicked directly into touch to make ground, except with a penalty kick (see below). In League the advantage will only go to the kicking side if the ball bounces on the playing side of the touch-line before going into touch.

A penalty kick can be taken in two ways. Either a player can place the ball on the ground to attempt a shot at goal or he can kick the ball directly into touch. If the second option is taken, the player can kick the ball either off the ground or out of his hands. If the ball goes into touch, the game is

Right: Penalty against this side. Below (left) Player penalized for dissent and below (right) scrum half illegally feeding his own forwards at a scrummage.

Above (left) obstruction. Above (right) hooker's foot up too early at scrummage. Left: Forward pass.

re-started with a tap kick opposite where the ball went out of play.

You will always know what is happening when the referee makes a decision because he makes a signal to the spectators to indicate the offence which has been penalized. There are 41 such signals and most of them make it quite plain which offence has happened. The touch-judges too have a limited number of signals which they make to indicate circumstances to the referee.

RULES CLINIC

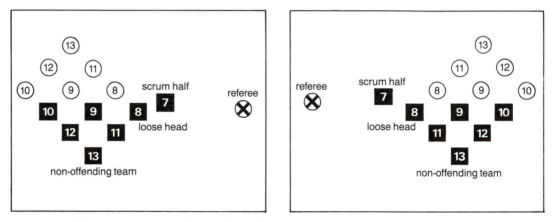

The placing for the forwards at the scrummage for each direction of play.

In the guide to the game it was mentioned that a triangle of forwards face each other in a scrummage. How do you decide which set of forwards have the advantage of the head on the outside?

In 1988, the International Board, the game's law-making body, decreed that in every scrummage – for whatever reason – the non-offending side will have the advantage of the prop forward nearest to the scrum-half.

What happens to a team after they have had six successive tackles against them?

They have to hand the ball over to the opposing team and the game is re-started with a play-the-ball. Professional teams hate giving the ball away without having a chance of regaining it so they usually opt to kick the ball after the fifth tackle. This has the effect of forcing the opposition to start their tackle sequence as far away from the kicker's line as possible; it also gives the kicking side the chance to regain possession if their opponents infringe or make a mistake under pressure from players who have followed up the kick downfield. If during the tackle sequence an opponent touches the ball in any way, the referee can order the count to start again.

Can a referee allow any advantage?

Most certainly. Although it is not written into the laws of the game the referees have total discretion. If it is obvious that the non-offending team can gain an advantage by play continuing, the referee can allow the game to carry on. And that does not mean that the offending player gets away with it. When the play sequence ends a referee can penalize him at that point.

If a ball drops on the touch-line is it in play or out?

In Rugby League the touch-line is counted as out of the field of play. The same applies to the touch-in-goal and the dead-ball lines. The goal-line counts as in-goal, and if a player grounds the ball on that line it counts as a try.

Are there any restrictions on the movements of players and can they all score?

The answers are no and yes. All 26 players on the pitch can move anywhere they wish and they can all score tries and goals.

How do the players know when to play the ball?

When an attacking player is not making progress in a tackle he has to play the ball but the referee will shout 'Held' indicating that the tackle is complete if there is any doubt. The defenders then have to retreat 5m (16ft) except for one man who will face the player in possession. Until the start of the

Side view of the forwards at a scrummage.

1988–89 season the defending player could be supported by a team-mate but, after a year-long experiment, it was disallowed. The attacker then places the ball down on the ground and drags it back with his foot to a team-mate behind him known as the 'acting half-back'. The defender may attempt to hook the ball back as soon as the ball touches the ground.

Is it possible to be ruled offside at a play-the-ball situation?

This is one of the biggest sources of dispute at any level of Rugby League. At the play-the-ball the referee will mark 5m (16ft) from the tackled players and the defenders must return to that mark. If they are caught encroaching, the referee will penalize the player concerned and award a penalty against him. If the ball is kicked downfield and players on the kicking side reach the player who catches it before his own team-mates can support him, they can be offside. They have to allow him either to kick the ball or run 5m (16ft) unhindered. Equally, if the player catching the ball fails to hold it and one of his team-mates grabs it without first getting behind the player who dropped it, he too would be offside.

In its simplest form you must be between your team-mate and your goal-line to receive the ball and remain onside. Offside is punishable by a penalty but if you are *accidentally* caught in an offside position, the referee can order a scrummage.

Previous page: Clash of the giants. Hull KR's Australian forward Peter Johnston meets with Castleford's Great Britain international forward Kevin Ward.

If a player about to score a try is badly obstructed or personally fouled, what happens?

Quite simply the referee awards the try if he is satisfied that the player concerned was certain to score. This is called a penalty try and no matter where the offence takes place it is always awarded under the posts, making life much easier for the goal-kicker. If the player is personally fouled during or just after the act of scoring the referee can award a penalty which is taken immediately after the conversion from in front of the posts.

What happens if a player is injured during the game?

Usually, injured players are treated on the field of play while the game continues. But if it is clear that by continuing the game the safety and well-being of that player would be endangered the referee can call a halt and stop the game-clock, making the necessary signal to the time-keepers. If after treatment a player in possession cannot immediately

A goal kick after a try has been scored.

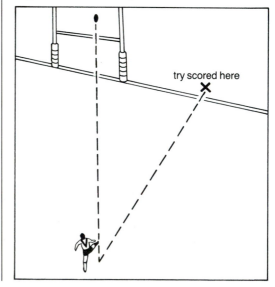

try scored here

play the ball the laws have now been adjusted so that he can hand the ball over to a team-mate to re-start the game.

Sometimes local dignitaries kick a match off. Does that count as the start of the game?

No, it does not! The ball must be returned to the centre-spot for the game to start with a proper kick-off.

If you have just scored a try does it matter where you place the ball for a conversion attempt?

Kickers have some discretion so that they can achieve a more favourable angle. They can place the ball at any point on an imaginary line running parallel with the touch-line from the place where the try was scored. A touch-judge will mark the position where the line has to start and when the kicker is ready to take his shot the official moves behind the posts.

For a goal to count the ball must completely cross the crossbar and be kicked on the full without being touched in flight by an opponent. Incidentally, unlike Rugby Union, in Rugby League it is illegal to distract the goal-kicker by charging at him during a conversion attempt. In the professional game touch-judges indicate if a goal-kick is successful but the referee is the sole judge. And his decision is final.

In Rugby League the game is sometimes re-started with a drop kick from under the posts. When does this happen?

In the Laws there are seven instances. Basically they all relate to happenings in the in-goal area. For example, if one of your players kicks a loose ball over the dead-ball line or touches down a loose ball in his own in-goal area this is the way to re-start play. It is also used if a defender infringes or is tackled in the in-goal area. If an attacker

infringes in the in-goal area or is the last to touch the ball before it goes over the dead-ball or touch-in-goal line, then the defending side can kick the ball off with a place kick at the 22-metre line. If, after an unsuccessful goal-kick the ball goes dead, the defending side can re-start with a drop kick from the centre of the 22-metre line.

Tackling is an essential part of the game. Is there any way you cannot ground an opponent?

Yes, despite its appearance the art of tackling is very disciplined. It has to be for the safety of all the players concerned. You are not allowed to use your knees or employ any special throws or holds, e.g. of a martial arts kind, which are liable to cause injury. You can use your leg to bring an opponent over providing your arms makes contact with him first.

How does a referee decide you have knocked the ball on?

The criteria for his decision are quite simple and straightforward. He will penalize you if he thinks that you have deliberately knocked the ball forward or passed forward. A knock-on is where you hit the ball with your hand or arm and it goes to ground.

If you fail to hold the ball and re-gather it after it goes to ground then the referee will award a scrummage with head and feed to your opponents. If, after knocking the ball on, it doesn't touch the floor or a goal-post or crossbar you will be allowed to carry on in possession. By the way, if you charge down an opponent's kick that will not be judged as a knock-on.

An attacking player passes the ball close to his opponent's line and it rebounds from his team-mate's head on to the floor. Can the first player re-gather and score?

Yes, the try stands. As long as his team-mate did not touch it with his hands or arms it does not matter from which part of the body the ball rebounds.

If a full-back catches the ball in the in-goal area can his opponents try to tackle or dispossess him?

Until recently they could. But, in view of the danger to any player up in the air trying to

Saved! A player prevents a knock-on by regathering the ball after it rebounds off his body.

catch a high kick under pressure from several attacking players, it was decided that if he held the ball cleanly he should remain unmolested and his skill should be rewarded

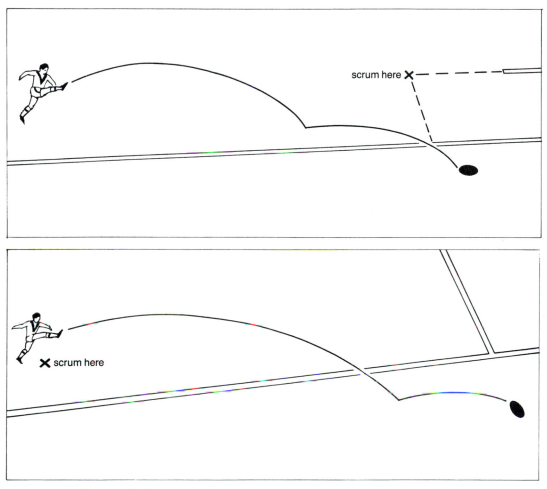

(Above) Finding touch. Note the ball bouncing before leaving the pitch.
(Below) Ball back. The kicker puts the ball directly out of play.

by being allowed to re-start the game with a tap kick on the 22-metre line.

As a player rises to play-the-ball he puts his foot on the touch-line. Can he continue?

Yes, he is allowed to play-the-ball.

If a referee sends a player to the sin bin how do you know when he will return to the game?

In Britain the referee will dismiss the player and then hold up a coloured card. The yellow card indicates a five-minute absence and the red card ten minutes. Alternately he can signal with five fingers or ten.

What happens if a player kicks the ball and it doesn't bounce before going into touch?

If the ball goes out on the full then it is brought back to where the kick was made and a scrum formed. If it bounces off a player following a kick then the scrum takes place where it hit him – or her.

If a player is tackled short of the line but slides into the in-goal area, does it count as a try?

Yes, it does. If his momentum following the tackle carries him over the line and he is neither in touch nor touch-in-goal then the score is good. If he comes to a halt in a tackle just before the line and then reaches over he will be penalized for making a second movement. Should the ball not be grounded then he could try to continue because the tackle was not complete.

How much power does a referee have in Rugby League?

Total control. He is appointed to be the guardian of the Laws and his control starts even before a player sets foot on the pitch. He is in charge of them from the moment they come into the playing area until the second they leave. Anybody else who wants to come on to the pitch must have his permission.

In professional Rugby he will have the help of two touch-judges but that is not always so in amateur games. He is the only official allowed to award tries or goals, although he

may take advice from a touch-judge if he is unsighted by the action of play. He has the power to suspend play for whatever reason, for example because of adverse weather conditions, undue interference from spectators, misbehaviour by the players or anything else which interferes with the game.

He has the authority to send players off the pitch for misbehaviour or persistent transgression of the laws. And he can dismiss them permanently or for temporary spells of five or ten minutes in the sin bin. He controls the game with the aid of a whistle and he will sound it for six reasons.

1 A try or goal has been scored.
2 The ball has gone out of play.
3 He sees a breach of the laws except when advantage applies.
4 If the ball or player comes into contact irregularly with the referee, touch-judge or anybody not officially connected with the game or an object which should not be on the pitch.
5 When anything not provided for in the Laws happens and a team gets an unfair advantage.
6 When a stoppage is necessary to enforce the Laws or for any other reason.

Once a referee has made a decision he cannot change it and that is why it is useless trying to pressurize him with dissent. The only exception to that situation is when a touch-judge reports an incident of foul play that the referee did not see before making his decision. Being a Rugby League referee is not an easy job. For example, he has to keep a count of the completed tackles while play is in motion, signal his decisions and carry a huge responsibility. To reach the level of the professional game he has to pass a series of examinations and reach either Grade 1 or 2. And, at each professional game, there will be an assessor who watches his performance and monitors the quality of his application of the laws.

Is there any occasion when you can kick the ball directly into touch?

Yes. When you are awarded a penalty. From that point, assuming it is not a differential penalty, there is a choice: a kick at goal for two points or the option of gaining ground. If you decide on the latter then you can put the

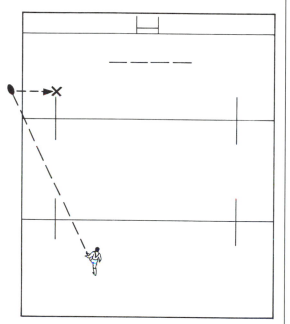

A penalty kick to the touchline.

ball into touch on the full and then re-start the game with a tap kick from the point level with where the ball went into touch.

If a team receives the ball after a 'hand-over' does the play-the-ball that re-starts the game count as one of their sequence?

No, it does not. The referee will start counting their conceded tackles from the moment the game is re-started. The referee will indicate when the sequence is coming to an end because at the fifth tackle he will put his hand straight up into the air and shout 'Last'. Then a team will have to decide

whether to kick the ball or risk another tackle and hand the ball over. If during a sequence the defending team touches the ball but fails to retain it, the referee can nullify the count and start again at once. A ricochet or rebound off a player does not count as a 'touch' and players cannot gain an advantage by kicking the ball against an opponent.

What is a differential penalty?

This penalty can only be awarded for a scrum offence and the only difference between it and a normal penalty is that you do not have the option of kicking at goal. To re-start the game the non-offending team has to kick the ball into touch or take a tap kick. But that does not mean that every offence at a scrummage will be punished with a differential penalty. The referee can still award a normal penalty against any player for foul play and offside.

Can you play the ball to yourself and play on?

Yes, provided that you are not being marked by an opponent.

Where does the non-feeding scrum half stand at a scrummage?

A new law was introduced at the start of 1988–89 which laid down that the non-feeding scrum half should retire behind the pack like all the other players not involved in the scrummage. All the payers outside the scrum must retire by 5m (16ft) until the ball has emerged.

What happens if a player is caught in an offside position through no fault of his own?

If the player concerned comes into contact with a ball carrier or the ball the referee can allow play to continue if no attempt is made to play or interfere with the game. But if the player in the off-side positions gains an advantage for his side a scrum must be formed with head and ball going to the non-offending team. The referee will not penalize the player for being accidentally offside. It is possible for a player to take possession of the ball and not realize that he is in an offside position; if the referee believes the player did not know he was offside, he can rule it as accidental.

Can you be offside in your own in-goal area?

You cannot be offside in your own in-goal area but you can be penalized in your opponent's.

If a trainer runs on to the field of play to treat an injured player and collides with an

attacking player, what happens?

The game must be re-started with a play-the-ball which does not count in the attacking team's sequence.

An attacking player kicks the ball ahead and a defender charges it down. The player who kicked re-gathers the ball and

Charging a kick down.

continues the attack. What is the referee's ruling?

The teams play on and the tackle count is set back, if necessary, to one in favour of the attacking team. If the defender had succeeded in holding the ball or gained possession of it, the referee would also have allowed the teams to play on. A charge-down of a kick does not count as a knock-on.

A player catches a penalty kick on the full but his foot is on the touch-line. What happens next?

The second phase of the penalty applies because the player who caught the ball was in touch. The line markings are out of play. If the player had caught the ball on the dead-ball line after it had been kicked during open play the defending team would have been given the ball to re-start the game with a place kick from the centre of the 22-metre line. The situation is judged to be the same as if the attacking team had kicked the ball dead behind their opponents' line.

If the hooter goes after the award of a penalty, can the kick still be taken?

If it is a place kick the team awarded the penalty have the option to kick at goal and the score would count. Alternatively they could choose the tap penalty and attempt to

score a try, which would count. The play in that case would only be ended if the defenders could complete a tackle before the attacking side scored.

If a player who has knocked the ball forward is prevented from picking it up by an opponent, will play continue?

No, because the team who lost possession will receive a penalty. You cannot obstruct an opponent not in possession, even one who is offside or trying to regain a ball that has been knocked on.

What happens if you kick at goal and the wind blows the ball back across the crossbar?

There's no need to worry because the goal still stands. As long as the whole of the ball crosses the bar the score has been correctly made.

Would the referee allow a try to be scored if during a scrum near the line the attacking side push over the goal-line and drop on the ball?

No, you cannot score in a scrummage. But if the ball comes out at the rear of the attacking side's pack and one of their players charges through the rest of his forwards to touch down then the try would be allowed.

TECHNIQUE

Rugby League is becoming increasingly popular because it demands great quantities of skill, fitness, courage and, most of all, teamwork. Whatever level of the game you come into contact with it is essential that you have some command of the techniques needed to play a useful part in a team effort. There will always be some players in a side who are blessed with more skills and talent than the rest but they are not likely to function properly if the other players in the team cannot fulfill the simple necessities of the game.

Broken down into basic requirements Rugby League players should be able to catch and run with the ball, pass it to a colleague and tackle. If you can perform all those functions adequately then the only other problem you have is choosing which position you are best suited to. Of course, when it comes to actually playing the game there is much more to consider, but without those three basic skills your progress and enjoyment of the game will be necessarily limited.

Each of those three elements can be performed at a basic level in your early matches. Once you have learned them, then you are in a position to develop them in such a way that you can add considerable variety and effectiveness to both the team's and

Australian Test scrum half Peter Sterling played for British club Hull in 1985 when they reached the Cup Final against Wigan. Unfortunately for this fine player he finished up on the losing side.

your personal performance. This is what we mean by technique. What you have to remember about Rugby League is that you have two distinct phases: attack, when you are in possession, and defence, when the opposition have the ball. Each phase requires different skills from the players and that is why it is so important to listen to your team coach or teacher. They have the advantage of being able to look on at a game and how your performance is fitting in.

The ball is in play for a considerable amount of time in Rugby League and it is important for you to pay great attention to your personal fitness. As well as ensuring that you will be able to last through the full 80 minutes, contributing all the time, being fit will also reduce your chances of serious injury. League is a hard, physical game – there is no disguising that fact – but you can reduce the risks to yourself if you are in good shape. Clearly, the higher up the ladder you go the more is asked of you in training. Professional players are given fitness programmes for the summer break while top amateur players in the élite National League train almost as hard as the professionals. At other levels, the requirements are more basic but just as important.

Tactics have always been important in Rugby League, and in the modern game with its limited number of tackles they have become even more crucial. The side who control the ball have a better than even chance of winning the game, so it follows that the team with the more skilful players are more likely to control possession for longer.

PASSING · & · HANDLING

The first skill you will need is to be able to pass the ball effectively in either direction. You are a passenger if you cannot give the ball to somebody else when you are tackled, or when a team-mate is better placed or in order to move the ball to a superior tactical position.

Once you have the ball in your hands you are the centre of attraction. Defenders will be looking either to stop you or make you drop it while your team-mates expect to receive a

(a) Pull the arms back when ready to pass and note the position of the feet when passing left. (b) Keep your eyes on the intended receiver.

good, accurate pass. It is essential to have a well-rehearsed, consistent grip on the ball. Imagine you are making a cradle shape with your hands and lower arms. Grip the ball with your fingers spread out on the under part while using your thumbs to hold on to the upper portion. Your arms should be relaxed and bent slightly from the elbow so that you can swing the ball in either direction. Your thumbs hold the ball securely in position and you should be able to move it up and down as well as across your body.

Now that you feel comfortable holding the ball, try running up and down the pitch with it so that you become accustomed to the action. Passing has two phases. First you have to deliver the ball to a team-mate. Assuming that you are holding it properly you have to take aim and this means that you have to keep an eye on the target. Years of experience show that the ideal place for a pass to be received is called the 'bread basket', located between the lower chest and waist.

Keeping your eye on that target, twist from the waist and swing your arms well back.

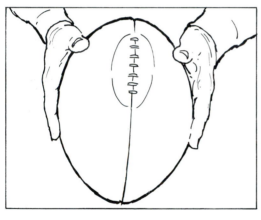

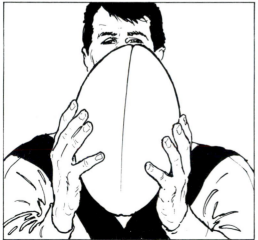

(Left above) How to hold the ball from above. See the thumb placings.
(Left below) Notice the spread of the fingers under the ball.

(a)

(b)

Now bring your arms back across your body and let the ball go towards the target area making sure that on release it travels in front of the man you are passing to. You will be able to direct the ball with your wrists and fingers, but bear in mind that the speed of your pass will be dictated by how far in front of the player you need to direct the ball. Clearly the faster he is going the more you must aim in front of him.

Once you have let the ball go, follow through with your arms so that they are fully extended towards the receiver with the fingers pointing at the target. Keeping this in mind helps both your action and direction.

That is one half of the art of passing. As well as giving passes you have to be able to receive them. It is no use being a member of any team if you cannot hold the ball regularly when it is passed to you. Once you think that a player is likely to pass the ball to you it is time to start your preparations. It may only take a fraction of a second but the same principles are always observed. First, you must not take your eye off your team-mate no matter what is going on around you. Move your arms and hands out with fingers extended to face the passer. It always helps if you use both hands but in some circumstances this is not possible. If you are forced to use one hand then apply the same method. Once the ball reaches you it should be brought into your body. This will help you bring it under control and prepare you to pass it on if required. If you grip the ball in the same way as you did when you were passing it, a tackler will find it less easy to dislodge.

There are two things to keep in mind. You must be ready to catch a badly directed pass and to receive the ball unexpectedly. Quite often the ball is released at an unlikely moment; if it surprises you, no doubt it will be doing the same to the opposition. By catching it cleanly, though, you retain possession and the initiative for your team.

When you come to deliver your passes during play, you will inevitably be running. When you are passing to the left you should aim to pass when the right leg is leading and vice versa when you move the ball to the right. This will give you more twist in your body and greater accuracy to your pass.

Experience and practice will teach you when a pass is necessary, and there is one golden rule which your team-mates will always appreciate your remembering. That is, 'Never pass to somebody in a worse position than yourself.' If your colleague is well marked it is better to absorb the tackle and seek a better position for your team after a play-the-ball. This is one reason why, once the ball is in your hands, you must be aware of the game around you. It is no use, for example, hanging on to the ball while the defence becomes organized. Think too of the possibilities offered by a long pass. You can sometimes take the opposition completely by surprise by lofting the ball over the head of your nearest team-mate to one

The dotted line shows a legal pass and one which is forward.

beyond. At the same time, though, a pass of that kind is easier to intercept, so you should only use it when you are certain of reaching your man.

Never forget that in Rugby you can only pass backwards. At first it can seem difficult but, after practice, it becomes second nature. In League the act of passing is not restricted to just running movements. You may be called upon to take up a position as acting half-back, and it is advisable to be proficient at passing from the ground. When you do this, make sure you know exactly where your receiver is and how much weight you will need to put into the pass. Bend well over the ball and, taking a firm grip, prepare to make the pass. Turn your body towards your receiver and pass from the ground, ensuring that you do not straighten your back but stay on your feet. Again the ball is directed with your fingers and wrists with a well-defined follow-through.

Not that you can always take the ball off the floor in such controlled circumstances. If you see a loose ball, the chances are that if

TECHNIQUE

Keep your eyes firmly fixed on the ball.

Now that long, high kicks have become common in the League game it is important that every player is able to deal with them. The art requires concentration, judgment and confidence. As soon as you see a high ball heading your way position yourself underneath and form your arms into a cradle with your fingertips facing the ball. When the ball makes contact with you,

Straddle the ball with your hands.

Grip the ball firmly and look at the player you want to find.

you run straight at it your boot will make contact first. Run alongside and scoop it up, running your hand underneath so that you can exert some grip at the same time. The key to the whole operation is concentration; keep your eye firmly fixed on the ball.

A bouncing ball represents a real problem. There is a saying in both codes of Rugby: 'Never let the ball bounce.' Because of its shape you can never tell which direction it will take. When you have to retrieve a ball that has bounced keep your eye on it all the time – it's the only chance you have.

(Left) Cradle your arms and watch the ball. (Right) Pull the ball into your chest, keeping your elbows together.

absorb the shock with your body and then wrap your arms around it. In other words, cuddle it. Keep your elbows in front of your body, although not too far apart or it will drop through the gap. Many players prefer

Ellery Hanley the Great Britain captain and one of the world's greatest players.

to jump to meet the ball. This is a decisive approach which needs care, co-ordination and plenty of practice.

PLAY-THE-BALL

The act of play-the-ball is a two-man scrummage. It is one of the distinctive plays that most people recognize as being particular to Rugby League and it has its own set of skills that players have to master.

The moment you are tackled in possession of the ball you have two choices. You can pass if you are still able to or you must absorb the tackle and play-the-ball. There are likely to be around 300 play-the-balls in a match, so it is a skill you cannot take lightly.

Speed is essential. A ball played slowly gives the opposition a chance to re-group and prepare for your team's next drive forward. Once the tackled player hits the ground or the referee calls 'Held', it is up to the ball-carrier to get to his feet as quickly as possible. He should lift the ball clear of the ground, taking care not to knock-on, and face his opponent's goal line. The next move is important. Bend well over the ball and place it lengthways on the floor next to your leading foot. Then release it. At the same time put your other foot on top of the ball and roll it back to the player who has taken up position behind you as acting half-back. The danger point for the ball-carrier is when the ball is placed on the ground because that is when the defending player can attempt to hook it away.

Playing-the-ball properly is essential in Rugby League. Hold the ball firmly as you place it on the ground, roll it firmly along the ground to the player behind and perform the movement as quickly as possible.

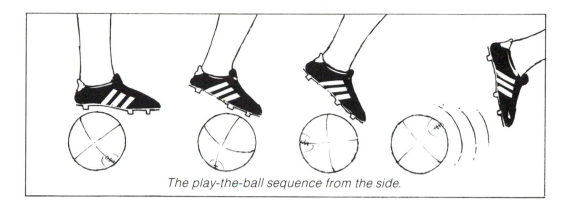

The play-the-ball sequence from the side.

Notice tackler's shoulder aimed at the thigh.
Opposite: Drive hard into the victim (top).
Head behind and legs bent for drive (centre).
Drive through to put victim off balance (bottom).

TACKLING

Having looked at how you play with the ball in your hands, now we must consider what happens when it is your turn to defend. Your team is now lined up across the pitch facing the opposition. It is your job to stop them breaking through and to ensure that they do not make progress while in possession. As a bonus you will be trying to dislodge the ball so that you can start an attack.

Tackling is not just a question of leaping on another player to inflict the maximum possible damage or pain. You have to be firm and resolute but not cruel. It also requires skill and courage to tackle properly without hurting yourself, and you should think about and practise your tackling regularly.

The objects of a tackle in Rugby League are three-fold. First, to stop the man making progress. Second, to prevent him from passing to a colleague and, third, to force him to lose possession. To achieve any of these three you must deliver your tackle with determination. The best way to go in is hard and low. When a player in possession is running towards you, put yourself in a position to intercept. Your target area is the thigh, and remember at all times to keep your head to one side of the ball-carrier. Drive your shoulder into the attacker and encircle his thighs with your arms. Once you have established a grip slide down the carrier's legs taking him to the ground. The tackler should end up on top of the carrier. If the tackle is done correctly the carrier will not have had time to release a pass and be forced to play-the-ball.

Clearly not every tackle will take place under perfect circumstances. In general, players have to make the contact from one of three directions: from the front, from the side and from behind. Each requires a slightly different method.

Front tackling (sometimes called head-on tackling)

There are two separate types of this tackle, the passive and the blockbuster. The first is when the tackler allows the ball-carrier to approach and then brings him down using the carrier's momentum to complete the tackle. Remember to position your head, allow the carrier virtually to run into you, drop your tackling shoulder and encircle his thighs. Once your grip is complete with your shoulder blocking his progress, apply pressure so that the attacker's own weight forces him to fall sideways.

In the blockbuster the target area for the tackler is the waist. The success of this tackle depends on your anticipation and speed of execution. When you spot the ball-carrier is in the position you have anticipated, move in quickly. Place your head alongside the player, grip under his centre of gravity, i.e. below his buttocks, and then pull and lift at the same time. Drive the ball carrier back and land on top with your shoulder in the target area.

Head-on tackling.
(Left) the power drive and (right) momentum tackle.

David Watkins, a Rugby League record breaker after his record signing from Welsh Rugby Union by Salford. He is still connected to the game as a broadcaster and commentator.

Rear tackle and side tackle

Once a player has broken through it is very likely that you will have to catch and tackle him from behind. Take care to stay away from his boots and use the method as described above. The side tackle is probably the easiest of the three to perform. Use the basic method and ensure you keep a grip on the carrier until he is well and truly grounded. Each time the target is the thigh.

Eyes fixed on target area for rear tackle.

Grip firmly round victim's thighs.

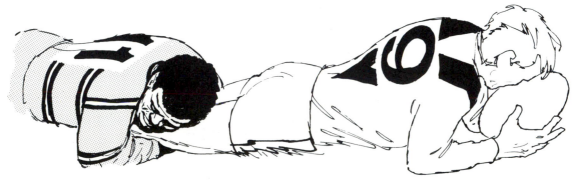

Smother tackle

Quite often in Rugby League there is not enough time to set up a proper tackle. When circumstances dictate that the ball-carrier should not be allowed to pass, that is the time to bring the smother tackle into play. Sometimes it is called the upright tackle because you attempt to prevent the player being in a position to release a pass while stopped in a standing position. When the carrier approaches, move forward and pin

Pin the ball between yourself and victim.

Drive through until victim is grounded.

the ball between yourself and the carrier's body. Your arms should be wrapped round the upper part of the carrier and his arms should be trapped by his side. It is important to realize that this tackle requires determination and timing so that the carrier is eventually forced to the ground.

KICKING

Although Rugby League is essentially a handling game, kicking is one of the most important and effective skills available to players and their teams. The simple act of kicking the ball forward can save the grind of driving it forward to gain ground, it can be used to score important points and relieve pressure in critical situations.

There are five ways to kick the ball in Rugby League.

Punt

If you kick the ball from the hands before it touches the ground it is called a punt. Hold the ball with one of its points aiming the way you are going to kick it. Keep your shoulders square with the target, ensure your head is down and that your eyes do not leave the ball until it is kicked. The ball should be held

a comfortable distance away from your body and the boot, when it makes contact, should fit into the rounded area of the ball. Keep the toes pointing forward and drive the foot through the ball. Remember that in broken play if you are looking to make ground then the ball must bounce before it goes into touch otherwise your team will have to return to the spot where the kick was made and concede the advantages of sight and feed at a scrum.

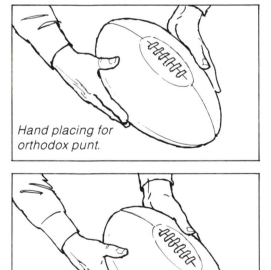

Hand placing for orthodox punt.

Positioning for drop kick.

Torpedo punt

The second variety of punt kick is called a torpedo. It receives its name because when the ball is kicked it spins through the air like a torpedo or bullet, helping the kicker gain valuable extra distance. To impart the spinning effect you must vary the normal punt technique. It is essential to hold the ball correctly – one hand should be placed marginally forward of the other, just under the ball, and it should be held slightly pointing inwards. This means that when you drop the ball it arrives at an angle across the instep; the kicking foot should also be angled inwards when it makes contact. As distance is the object, you should avoid kicking the ball too high, remembering that the spin causes the ball to curve in the air.

Body position ready for punt kick (left), notice how the ball fits nicely in the arc of the foot (below) and the essential good follow through (right).

Grubber kick

This useful little kick sends the ball along the ground in advance of your team. It allows your team-mates to run through with a chance of regaining possession while, at the same time, making life very difficult for the defenders trying to gather it up. Hold the ball as if you were going to pass and guide it along the floor with your foot. Make sure that your body is over the ball and send if off with a stabbing kick with no follow-through.

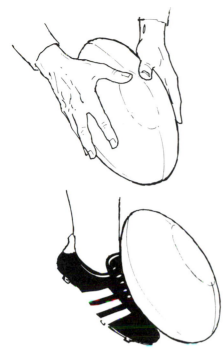

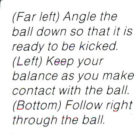

(Far left) Angle the ball down so that it is ready to be kicked. (Left) Keep your balance as you make contact with the ball. (Bottom) Follow right through the ball.

Kick-over

Tactically, this is a lofted variant of the grubber kick. Use the same stabbing action to punt the ball over the heads of the defenders. As before, avoid following through to keep the kick short.

Drop kick

Using the same principles as for the punt, the drop kick requires a slight variation in timing because the ball must hit the ground before contact is made. Take care to select your target area and then switch your attention to the kicking area where the ball will be dropped. Hold the ball clear of your body in the same way as you did to pass

Joe Lydon, a Great Britain international three-quarter. He was the first player to appear in the schoolboy curtain raiser game before the Cup Final at Wembley and then return as a professional. He has winners' medals with Widnes and Wigan.

and then adjust it to an angle of around 45 degrees relative to the ground. Try to place the ball near the toe of the non-kicking boot and then, with the lower part of the instep, kick the ball. Keep your head and eyes down all the time, spread your arms to help balance and lean slightly back so that your kick gains sufficient height to clear the crossbar. At a re-start, where the length of the carry is more important, delay the actual kick by a fraction.

Place kick

In this kick the ball is always played from the ground. It is generally used either to re-start a game or to kick at goal and the action should be tailored to suit the circumstances.

Kicking to start a match or re-start it after a score requires work with a team coach. The delivery of the kick has to be measured so that it meets your forwards who are arriving to challenge the opposition for possession. The kick at goal is a precision kick at a still target which, if successful, brings two valuable points for a conversion or a penalty. Both types of kick carry a lot of responsibility and as many team members as possible should practise and be prepared to take place kicks for their side.

There are two methods for place kicking. The first, and more traditional, involves kicking with the toe after a straight-on approach to the ball. The other involves kicking with the instep in a style known as 'round the corner'.

A common factor in both methods is that the ball is teed up like a golf ball. Many British goalkickers now prefer to have sand brought on each time they have an attempt at goal, using the sand to make a mound on which to tee the ball. This method became popular after it had been used for many years in Australia and New Zealand. The traditional British method is to make a hole in the turf and build up a tee from the soil. Both have the same effect: they set the ball up for the kicker.

(Above) Place ball firmly on ground with seam facing target. (Right) Ensure one foot is placed alongside ball.

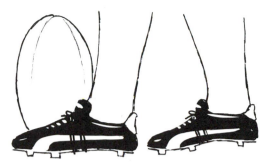

Notice the different angle of the ball.

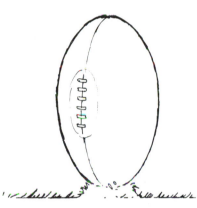

The ball placed on a mound of sand or soil ready for place kick.

*(Far left) Keep your eye on the ball.
(Left) Kick through the ball.*

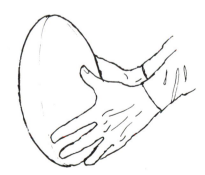

Using the elevated angle requires careful preparation.

Kickers have another choice. They can place the ball on the tee in an upright position, or make it lean slightly backwards or use the bullet style, laying the ball virtually flat on the tee with one end pointing at the target. The bullet method requires great care with lining up and it helps to have a seam running the length of the ball facing in the direction of the target. The kicker has to be very careful that he keeps body, ball and target all in a straight line.

The toe-end kicking method has considerable advantages for the beginner. The target, the ball and the player are in a straight line and that makes aiming easier. It is important that only the toe strikes the ball or there can be no guarantee of direction.

No matter which way the ball is placed the same method of approach to the kick is recommended. Once you have mastered your approach to the ball you can concentrate entirely on accuracy. Tee the ball up so that a central point, no more than 2.5 cm (1 in) from the bottom of the ball, is visible. This is called the spot. Aim a seam of the ball at the target while you are bending over to place the ball. Ensure that you, the ball and the target are in a straight line. Stand directly behind the ball and then place your non-kicking foot by the side of it. This is the moment for your last visual check to see that everything is in line. Keeping your eye on the ball, look at the spot referred to above. Concentrate on that spot until the ball is kicked. Now you should step back however many steps you want for your run-up; at the end of the run-up you pause, then with a rhythmic run approach the ball. When you arrive at the ball your non-kicking foot should return to its earlier place beside the ball. When your body is directly over the ball, your toe should make contact with the spot. Allow your foot to follow through and spread your arms to provide the necessary balance.

In the 'round the corner' method you kick the ball soccer-style using the upper part of the instep. That means you have more of the ball to aim at and you can wear lighter-weight boots. The problem, however, is that the trajectory of the ball is curved and a right-footed kicker on the right-hand side of the field finds it naturally difficult to hit the ball on-target. Some teams solve the problem by having one right- and one left-footed kicker.

Instep-kickers begin with the same method of approach, then after stepping out their run-up take a couple of paces to the right or left so that the run-up, apart from the last couple of strides, is curved. It is important to remember those last two steps because they line the kicker up with the target.

SCRUMMAGE

The scrummage is the chief unit skill in Rugby League. While the game is often, and justifiably, criticized for its untidy scrums there is a design to them that is not always visible or appreciated by spectators and television viewers. Increasingly over the last two or three seasons more attention has

The correct method for scrum halves to feed a scrummage.

Forwards set for a scrummage. Notice the binding of the arms.

been given to its potential, as demonstrated by successive Australian and New Zealand touring teams, and it is important to include scrummage technique regularly in coaching and training sessions.

It has been said that front-row forwards play their own private game within the match, and there is some truth in this. The whole point of the scrummage is to decide possession for the next play and, because holding the ball is so important, the skill, strength and determination of the front-row trio are crucial.

These three forwards provide a solid platform by binding their arms round each other and then interlocking heads with the opposing front-row forwards. This creates a clear tunnel into which the scrum-half will feed the ball. The moment the ball enters the tunnel the two hookers strike for it using one of their feet; possession is decided when one succeeds in dragging the ball back into his half of the scrummage. The two second-row forwards bind together with their arms and put their heads into the two gaps between the prop forwards and the hooker. Likewise the loose forward places his head between the two second-row forwards.

A useful tactic for the open-side prop is to lift his shoulder on the outside of the scrum so that his hooker can have a clear view of the ball at the feed. This has the effect of giving the scrum a humped appearance but is legal provided the binding between the players is maintained.

Before the put-in the players' bodies should be almost horizontal to the ground from the waist up, and in a pushing position. The scrummage is then ready to receive the ball. The scrum-half whose team has been awarded the put-in, re-starts play on the instruction of the referee. Because winning

Roger Millward, a legendary halfback for Hull KR and Great Britain who has also had a success as a coach.

possession at the scrummage is so important, your scrum-half and front-row forwards should regularly practise the put-in procedure using verbal and other signals to indicate when the ball is likely to enter the tunnel. This gives the hooker an advantage over his opposite number because he will know precisely when the feed is going to happen.

As a unit the forwards should be trained to deliver concerted pushes once the ball is fed into the scrum. A good push, linked to a strike by the hooker, is the best way to be sure of winning the ball. Once the hooker has taken the ball it should be channelled between the second-row forwards to the rear of the scrum. After it has gone through the second row the ball is in play and the scrum-half can pick it up.

The scrummage is a physically demanding set-piece and forwards should be fit enough to cope with its pressures. Upper-body strength is clearly an asset, linked to the stamina required to last and be effective for the full 80 minutes of a match.

TACTICAL
USE · OF · SKILLS

Once players have an understanding of the basic skills they can settle down to enjoy playing the game. Now they are ready to learn the extra individual skills that make a team member into a Rugby player.

Acceleration

You do not run at a single speed. You can vary your pace to suit every circumstance. For wingers particularly, the injection of sudden extra pace can be devastating. A defender believes that he has you trapped, and then you leave him stranded by accelerating away from him. The ability to vary your pace during a run always makes it more difficult for the defenders.

Bump-off

This is a skill that will help prevent ball-carriers being successfully tackled. As the defender comes in to make the tackle, the carrier should use a hard part of the body, the shoulder in particular, to bump-off the opponent. When using the chest players should fold their arms over the ball so that the brunt of the collision is taken on the forearm.

Swerve

The ball-carrier always has the advantage of knowing what he wants to achieve and can throw off potential tacklers with the gentle art of deception. Footwork is the key to a successful swerve, and timing is critical. Imagine a tackler coming in from the left. At the last moment you move to the right, balancing on the outside of your right foot and the inside of the left foot as you run. This takes you away from the tackler. To swerve left, simply reverse the balance points.

Dummy

Every Rugby player in the world at some stage in his career has bought, as they say, a dummy. That means they have been left stranded by another player who has fooled them into thinking he was going to pass and then did not.

The player in possession holds the ball

Preparing to bump-off a tackler.

A well-placed hand-off can prevent a successful tackle.

out as if he was going to pass to a team-mate. He goes through the motions of passing and then, at the last possible moment, holds on to the ball. The secret of selling a dummy is to catch the eye of the defender. He sees you setting up the pass and then sets off in pursuit of where he thinks the ball has gone.

Hand-off

This is called the fend- or palm-off in Australia and is used by ball-carriers when they are attempting to keep a tackling player at bay. The carrier switches the ball to one hand and pushes the defender off with the other. It should not be executed too early or the tackler will be able to take avoiding action. You should aim the palm of your hand – not your fist, that is foul play – towards your opponent's forehead, chest or shoulder and then deliver a firm push.

Sidestep

If you are advancing as a ball-carrier straight at a tackler who is bent down and in position to tackle you one of the best ways of beating him is by side-stepping. As you arrive within the tackler's range simply drive your left foot into the turf with all your weight on your toes. This brings your speed down dramatically and allows you to switch your weight to the right. To side-step left, reverse the pattern.

Then take a long stride to the right. The moment the right foot touches the ground push on it and take your left leg straight through, continuing your run. You should develop the skill so that you can sidestep in both directions. If you can only go one way other players will be able to anticipate your ploy. When executed properly the sidestep leaves tacklers groping at shadows.

Extra man and overlap

When you are playing against a team who can tackle well you have to create scoring chances either by penetrating their line with some of the running ploys we have just described or by outflanking them. If you

Determination can take you through a tackle.

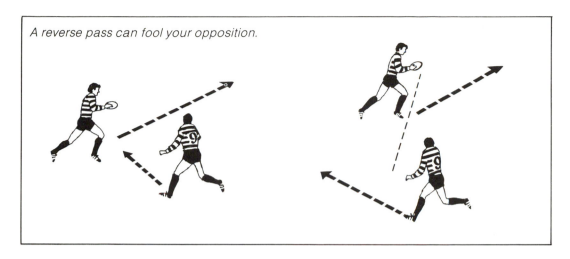

A reverse pass can fool your opposition.

merely pass the ball along the line to the winger the movement will break down when he is tackled by his opposite number. If, however, your full-back forsakes his defensive role and joins the three-quarter line as they attack there will be an extra attacker available at the end who can beat the defence.

The overlap can also be achieved by one player such as a centre three-quarter pulling one or two opposing three-quarters out of position by forcing them to tackle him and then passing the ball to a team-mate.

Support play

In Rugby League you can never hope to beat every tackle in every game. On many occasions it is to your team's advantage if you take the tackle and, before you are grounded, pass to a player coming in behind you. It is very little use if, every time you get the ball, you just charge forward into the tacklers. If you drive forward with several of your team-mates following it means that, even if you are stopped, the movement can continue if you pass the ball. A general rule

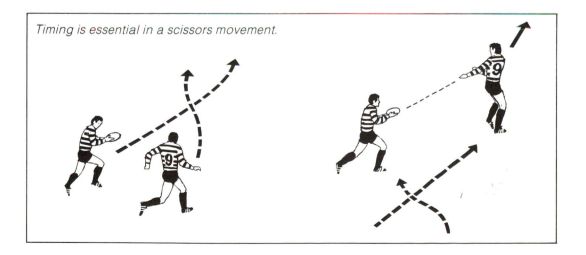

Timing is essential in a scissors movement.

for all League players is: 'Support the ball carrier'. You can never tell when a defensive error or scoring chance is going to happen.

Kick ahead

Against a defensive line that is lying flat, marking the attacking side man-for-man, a short kick ahead can break through the line and give the advancing attackers a chance to continue pressing home their advance. A cross-field kick behind the defenders to your wing, especially when used with a pre-arranged signal, can be very effective because it turns the defence and has them running back towards their line.

Reverse pass

In Rugby League it is often an advantage to switch the direction of play at the last possible second, and a most important part of that operation is the reverse pass. It can be performed in two distinct ways. First, the passer can turn his body virtually to face his own goal line and look at the receiver who will move inside and behind him. The ball is then simply transferred in the usual way in the direction of the receiver's run, and the advantage of this method is that the passer never loses sight of the player to whom he is giving the ball.

The second is a more complicated method which requires a great deal of understanding between team mates. The passer continues upfield towards the opponent's try-line and, as he runs, slips the ball up and behind him ensuring that he runs in front of the receiver. The receiver collects the ball at the last possible second and changes the direction of the attack.

Scissors

As one player moves diagonally across the field in one direction he passes the ball to a team-mate going in the opposite direction. This works best if the delivery can be

disguised until the last moment and the ball is 'smuggled' away. As with all passing moves, the more you practise the better you play.

Up-and-under or bomb kick

When you reach the fifth tackle and are close to your opponents' line, one of the best ways to create a scoring chance is to loft a very high punt. It puts considerable pressure on the defenders who may then make a mistake and concede possession.

Recent law changes mean that there is no advantage in kicking directly into the in-goal area around the goal-posts because if the full-back catches the ball cleanly he can re-start the game in possession with a

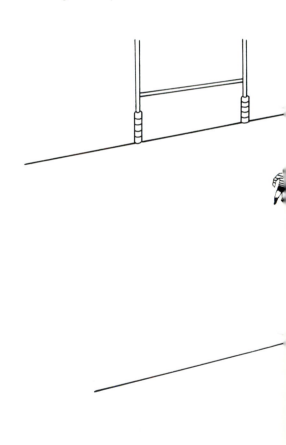

22-metre tap kick. Some professionals have found that they gain more by kicking across the field of play.

POSITIONAL · PLAY

One of the most important terms you are likely to hear in modern Rugby League is 'game-plan'. Basically it refers to the plan of campaign your coach has devised before the match. From what he knows and has learned about the opposition, he has thought of various methods of exposing their weak points. This means that your game becomes easier to organize on the field of play because you know both your team and individual targets. Of course, plans can change and there is always room for individual flair, but as playing standards rise the need for pre-planning becomes more necessary.

In Rugby League, and in Rugby Union for that matter, the players' positions remain the same wherever the game is played. A country may change the name it gives to a position or move but the essence of each player's job remains identical. Unlike soccer, where team formations vary between 4-2-4, 4-3-3, 4-4-2, etc., the layout of a Rugby team remains constant.

This means that it is possible to give a firm definition and responsibility to each position.

The full-back has so many attacking options and can cover all the gaps in the defensive line.

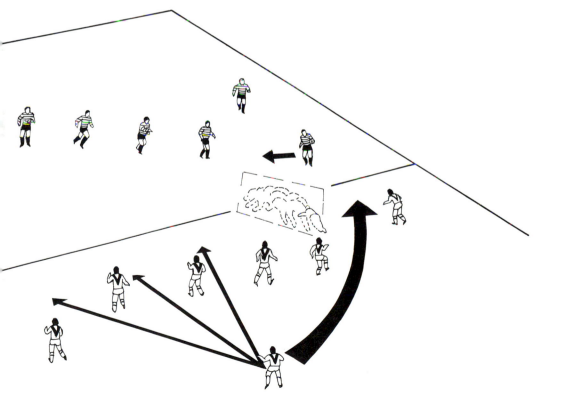

It is important that these roles are understood by the whole team because a successful outfit depends on each player knowing what is required of him and how his role fits in with those of his team-mates. Understandably too, every team member wants to think that he can rely on everyone else once the action starts.

Full-back

He is the last line of defence and can also be the first of attack. The full-back stands at the rear of the team and must be both a sure handler of the ball and a sound tackler. In modern Rugby League the high kick deep into the opponents' half is used frequently to seek out weak points and force defensive errors. In defence the full-back has to be a confident catcher and be able to gather the ball safely from the ground. When he is called upon to tackle it is usually in critical circumstances and he must be proficient at taking players to the ground or preventing them from passing.

That is one half of the full-back's role. Because he plays so deep in the defence he has a great overall view of the game and can judge either the perfect moment to link up with his three-quarter line as the extra man in attack or to pick the ideal spot for a penetrating kick into the opposition half. For that reason many of the top full-backs in Rugby League tend to be very proficient kickers both from the ground and tactically.

Wing three-quarter

There are two wingers in each team, left and right. It is a highly individualistic role. Their main function is to use speed and strength to score tries and they are also expected to add tackling support when the situation demands, for example in covering across if an opponent breaks away. Each wing has his own way of doing his job but, in general, there are two varieties of winger. One, usually a player with extra speed, will try to create space and time with elusive running, calling on side-steps, swerves and dummies while the second, usually a more robust type of player, will employ straight, powerful running with changes of pace and bump-offs in his path to the goal-line.

Centre three-quarter

The centre occupies one of the most interesting attacking positions on the team. He carries great responsibility and as part of the team's main attacking machinery he has a two-fold role.

He can either utilize his own individual skills and score himself or create dangerous situations that draw defenders in to meet him thereby creating space on the outside for a well-timed pass to reach an unmarked winger. The position is usually given to players who read the game well, and have pace and strength. Because most of their play is carried out at speed, centres should possess a good understanding with each other and with their wing men and stand-off half. Some teams prefer to operate a system where the same centre operates next to the stand-off half all through the game; he is generally known as the inside centre and his partner is the outside centre. More often, however, centres operate at left and right covering zones of the pitch. Good tackling ability is essential for centres who must resist the many attacking thrusts aimed through the middle of the three-quarter line.

Stand-off half

The stand-off must have great tactical awareness. He controls the ball supply to the backs and on his shoulders rests the decision when and how to attack through the three-quarters. He should also be able to take the initiative himself and for this he needs speed off the mark as well as tactical knowledge. He should be adept at evasive running and have good handling skills. This is one of the most demanding roles in the game and it is not surprising that a great stand-off can have an enormous impact on the game. The Australian players Brett Kenny and Wally Lewis are fine examples of men who have achieved super-star status in the world game.

Scrum-half

More often than not the scrum-half is the smallest man on the team. Many make up for this by being among the giant-sized characters of the game. He is selected for his agility and dexterity while, at the same time, he has to be extremely durable because of the number of tackles he has to perform and absorb. It is a position where individual skills count a great deal and he has tremendous impact on the game as a whole.

His main role is to act as a liaison between the forwards and the rest of the backs; within that definition however, he has a great deal of licence. He usually sees more of the ball than any other player in the team and, because of that, takes more responsibility. He can spoil a game plan by holding on to the ball and attempting too much on his own. His main job is to provide the three-quarters with a fast, efficient service from behind the scrum. In addition, like those top men in the professional game, Andy Gregory of Great Britain and Peter Sterling of Australia, he can dictate the whole pattern of the game through his individual skills.

The forwards' role in the scrummage has already been discussed but their contribution to the game goes far beyond that. They play a hugely important part in open play and their command of their positional jobs is of utmost importance to the team.

Loose or lock forward

Like the Queen in chess, the loose forward is a very versatile player. He is usually the first player away from a scrummage and has to

provide solid support for the scrum-half and the rest of the back division. It is an advantage if the loose forward has good pace because he is often used as one of the main runners through the gaps that appear in defence on either the open or blind side of a scrummage.

At the base of the scrum he works in tandem with the scrum-half, releasing possession after a scrum when he believes the moment is right for his half-back and acts as a defensive screen to prevent defenders reaching the scrum half. In defence a great deal is expected from the loose forward. He should constantly cover the player in possession, and this requires high levels of fitness and mobility.

Second-row forward

The second-row forwards are beasts of burden and the term 'engine room of the team' describes them perfectly. They are usually highly mobile players who spend a great deal of time carrying the ball at the opposition and tackling. At play-the-ball situations it is often the second-row men who are called upon to run at first man off the acting half-back as well as making themselves available in broken play to carry the ball as far as possible. One of the most useful assets of a second-row forward is a talent for backing up, and that means being constantly available to any player in possession, ready in case they are tackled and want to pass. Defensively, a second-row forward has to be constantly involved and his tackle-count at the end of the match should be among the highest recorded.

Prop forward

Physically, prop forwards need to be among the largest members of the side. Their role in the scrum requires power, and they play important roles in the attacking and defensive effort outside the set pieces. Many prop forwards combine their power with a great ball-handling skill to compensate for their lack of blistering pace. They can create openings for other players by taking the tackles and holding off the moment when they are brought down long enough to release the ball to a player who is free to continue the attack.

Props share the general duties of driving the ball upfield and supporting other players. The blind-side prop usually makes a big contribution to the tackle workload. Some props, like New Zealand's Kurt Sorensen who plays for English club Widnes, also possess pace and can be devastating on a wide run while others have made their names as goal-kickers. In a sharp burst, most props can create large holes in a defence if their runs are timed well off short-range passes.

Hooker

Once he is released from his scrummaging duties the hooker is now expected to add considerably to both attack and defence. In the past he trundled from scrum to scrum and, as long as he won the ball, that was all that was required of him. Today, he is a versatile player, often used as the acting half-back. Great Britain's Kevin Beardmore is a good example of today's super-mobile hooker who can dictate the pattern of play after a play-the-ball. In addition, of course, he has to share the more everyday ball-carrying and tackling duties with the rest of the pack.

USEFUL
ADDRESSES

Australian Rugby Football League
19th Floor, CAGA House
8-18 Bent Street
SYDNEY 2000, NSW

Postal address:
Box 4415, GPO,
Sydney,
Australia 2001

British Amateur Rugby League Association
Britannic Building
3 Upperhead Row
Huddersfield
W Yorkshire HD1 2JL

Fédération Française de Jeu à Treize
7 Rue Jules Breton
75013 Paris
France

New Zealand Rugby Football League
CPO Box 712
Auckland 1
New Zealand

Papua New Guinea Rugby Football League
PO Box 1095
Boroko

Rugby Football League
180 Chapeltown Road
Leeds LS7 4HT

United States Rugby League
PO Box 56153
Madison
Wisconsin, 53705
USA

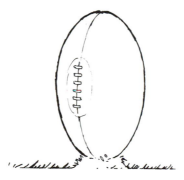

RULES CLINIC
INDEX

Alex Murphy, believed by many people to have been one of the greatest players ever produced by Rugby League. Has also achieved success as a coach to several major British clubs.

INDEX